# FLORIDA TEST PREP

# Language & Editing

# FSA Quiz Book

# Grade 4

ISBN 978-1500971342

# CONTENTS

# INTRODUCTION
# For Parents, Teachers, and Tutors

This workbook will develop all the language skills that students in Florida need and prepare students for the Florida Standards Assessments (FSA). It includes revising and editing exercises that require students to apply language skills, as well as quizzes that focus specifically on each language skill that students are expected to have. This workbook covers the skills listed in the Language Arts Florida Standards (LAFS) that were adopted in March 2014.

## Preparing for the Florida Standards Assessments (FSA)

In 2014-2015, Florida introduced new state tests to replace the FCAT 2.0 assessments. These are the Florida Standards Assessments (FSA). Language and vocabulary skills are assessed on the test in two ways. The test includes language and editing tasks where students read short passages and identify errors or opportunities for improvement. These tasks make up between 15 and 25 percent of the questions. Language and vocabulary skills are also assessed as part of the reading comprehension tasks, with some of the questions following passages covering language and vocabulary use. This book will prepare students for both types of questions, as well as ensure that students have the specific language skills that are assessed.

## Section 1: Revising and Editing Quizzes

Section 1 of this book focuses on editing and revising. It contains 4 sets of 5 passages. Each passage includes errors or opportunities for improvement. The questions following each passage require students to identify errors that need to be corrected, to identify ways that the passage can be improved, or to apply language skills based on the passage.

This section of the book gives students the opportunity to apply language skills in context. Students answer questions similar to those found on the language and editing sections of the FSA English Language Arts test.

## Section 2: Language, Vocabulary, and Grammar Quizzes

Section 2 of this book contains individual quizzes focused on each of the language skills that students need. It covers the skills specifically described in the Language section of the Language Arts Florida Standards, as well as the skills described in the Foundational Skills of the Reading standards. By focusing on each skill individually, students will gain a full and thorough understanding of the skill. As well as developing and improving language skills, this section will enhance reading and writing skills.

# Section 1
# Revising and Editing
# Quizzes

# Revising and Editing Quizzes

# Set 1

---

**Instructions**

Read each passage. Each passage is followed by questions.

For each multiple-choice question, read the question carefully. Then select the best answer. Fill in the circle for the correct answer.

For other types of questions, follow the instructions given.

---

## Building Your Vocabulary

As you read the passages, list any words you do not understand below. Use a dictionary to look up the meaning of the word. Write the meaning of the word below.

Word: _____

Meaning: _____

_____

Word: _____

Meaning: _____

_____

Word: _____

Meaning: _____

_____

Word: _____

Meaning: _____

_____

Word: _____

Meaning: _____

_____

# Quiz 1

**Read the passage below. Then answer the questions that follow it.**

## Monday

"Wow, that thing is annoying!" Kensi blurted out from her bed, as her hand slammed down on the alarm's snooze button.

"How on earth can it be six in the morning already?" she mumbled to herself.

After a long weekend of having fun with her friends, Kensi wasn't feeling anywhere near ready to start class's again. Kensi was slowly slipping away back to sleep when the alarm buzzed again.

BLARP, BLARP, BLARP!

Kensi jumped in shock. She buried her head into the pillow and pulled the blankets over her head, but there was no escape from the sound. She finally reached over and turned her alarm off, reluctantly getting out of bed. She stretched her arms and yawned.

"I really don't like Mondays!" Kensi muttered.

1    The author uses the words "slammed down" to describe how Kensi turns off the alarm. What do these words suggest about how Kensi feels?

_____

_____

_____

_____

**2**   The word *reluctant* means "unwilling." What does the word *reluctantly* mean?

    Ⓐ    in an unwilling way

    Ⓑ    someone who is unwilling

    Ⓒ    more unwilling

    Ⓓ    to cause to become unwilling

**3**   In the first sentence, what does the word *thing* refer to?

    Ⓐ    the bright morning sun

    Ⓑ    the alarm clock

    Ⓒ    the snooze button

    Ⓓ    the pillow on the bed

**4**   Which word could replace the word *muttered* in the last sentence without changing the meaning of the sentence?

    Ⓐ    explained

    Ⓑ    grumbled

    Ⓒ    screamed

    Ⓓ    laughed

**5**   Which change should be made in the third paragraph?

    Ⓐ    Change *friends* to *freinds*

    Ⓑ    Change *class's* to *classes*

    Ⓒ    Change *slowly* to *slowing*

    Ⓓ    There is no change needed.

## Quiz 2

**Read the passage below. Then answer the questions that follow it.**

### First Day

The siren blared and all of the officers started running around the locker room.

"Woop! Woop! We have an emergency call. Corner of George Street. Woop! Woop!" came over the Loudspeaker.

It was Chris's first day on the job and he was noticeably anxious.

"Suit up, Rookie. We've got you every step of the way!" Sergeant Carter yelled as he was pulling on his vest.

Chris nodded and finished gearing up. He began feeling a little more confidenter he could get through his first day.

1    Idioms are phrases that have special meanings. The meaning is not based on the usual meanings of the words. The idiom "every step of the way" means "at all times." Write the meaning of the common idioms below.

   to call it a day

   _____

   to be under the weather

   _____

   to be a pain in the neck

   _____

**2**    Which word from the passage does NOT need to start with a capital letter?

Ⓐ    George

Ⓑ    Street

Ⓒ    Loudspeaker

Ⓓ    Sergeant

**3**    The phrase "suit up" is used to tell Chris to –

Ⓐ    calm down

Ⓑ    put on his uniform

Ⓒ    get out of the way

Ⓓ    ask for help

**4**    Which sentence from the passage is NOT a complete sentence?

Ⓐ    *We have an emergency call.*

Ⓑ    *Corner of George Street.*

Ⓒ    *We've got you every step of the way!*

Ⓓ    *Chris nodded and finished gearing up.*

**5**    Which change should be made in the last sentence?

Ⓐ    Change *began* to *begun*

Ⓑ    Change *little* to *littel*

Ⓒ    Change *confidenter* to *confident*

Ⓓ    Change *through* to *threw*

# Quiz 3

**Read the passage below. Then answer the questions that follow it.**

## Pigeons

(1) Within the animal kingdom, Columbidae is the bird family consisting of species of doves and pigeons. (2) Doves and pigeons are solid-bodied birds with short necks and short slender bills. (3) Dove is generally the name given to the smaller birds. (4) Pigeons are usually larger. (5) The species of the Columbidae family most people are familiar with is the rock pigeon. (6) It is also known as the domestic pigeon. (7) They are common in many cities throughout the world.

(8) Rock pigeons once lived mainly on sea cliffs. (9) They have adapted well to city life. (10) Many people find city life stressful. (11) Pigeons use buildings as a form of cliff, and are often seen on window ledges, on the tops of buildings, and on structures such as bridges. (12) They often feed on food scraps. (13) They tend to congregate together in large groups. (14) Pigeons are considered by many to be pests, especially in cities.

1    Which of these shows the best way to combine sentences 3 and 4?

    (A)    Dove is generally the name given to the smaller birds, while pigeons are usually larger.

    (B)    Dove is generally the name given to the smaller birds, therefore pigeons are usually larger.

    (C)    Dove is generally the name given to the smaller birds, except pigeons are usually larger.

    (D)    Dove is generally the name given to the smaller birds, yet pigeons are usually larger.

**2**  Which sentence does NOT belong in the passage?

&#9398;  Sentence 6

&#9399;  Sentence 10

&#9400;  Sentence 12

&#9401;  Sentence 14

**3**  Which word could replace the word *congregate* in sentence 13?

&#9398;  hide

&#9399;  fight

&#9400;  gather

&#9401;  chat

**4**  Which transition word would be best to add to the start of sentence 9?

&#9398;  However,

&#9399;  Nearly,

&#9400;  Likewise,

&#9401;  Finally,

**5**  Where would be the best place to add the sentence below?

**Doves and pigeons have small heads compared to their bodies.**

&#9398;  Before sentence 1

&#9399;  After sentence 2

&#9400;  After sentence 5

&#9401;  After sentence 7

## Quiz 4

**Read the passage below. Then answer the questions that follow it.**

### The Violet
By Jane Taylor

Down in a green and shady bed
A modest violet grew;
Its stalk was bent, it hung its head,
As if to hide from view.

And yet it was a lovely flower,
No colors bright and fair;
It might have graced a rosy bower,
Instead of hideing there.

Yet there it were content to bloom,
In modest tints arrayed;
And there diffused its sweet perfume,
Within the silent shade.

Then let me to the valley go,
This pretty flower to see;
That I may also learn to grow
In sweet humility.

1    Adjectives are describing words. List all the adjectives used in the first
stanza.


_____       _____


_____       _____

**2**   Which word in the second stanza is spelled incorrectly?

Ⓐ   lovely

Ⓑ   bright

Ⓒ   instead

Ⓓ   hideing

**3**   Which change should be made in the line below?

**Yet there it were content to bloom,**

Ⓐ   Change *there* to *their*

Ⓑ   Change *were* to *was*

Ⓒ   Change *bloom* to *blooming*

Ⓓ   There is no change needed.

**4**   Which word in the first line of the last stanza is a pronoun?

Ⓐ   let

Ⓑ   me

Ⓒ   the

Ⓓ   valley

**5**   In which line is a simile used to describe the violet?

Ⓐ   *A modest violet grew;*

Ⓑ   *Its stalk was bent, it hung its head,*

Ⓒ   *As if to hide from view.*

Ⓓ   *And yet it was a lovely flower,*

## Quiz 5

**Read the passage below. Then answer the questions that follow it.**

### Albertosaurus

The Albertosaurus was a carnivorous dinosaur that lived around 65 million years ago. The Albertosaurus was discovered after fossils were found in Alberta, Canada. This discovery was first made on June 9 1884. The dinosaurs were thought to live only in north america.

The Albertosaurus looked simalar to its famous relative the tyrannosaurus. However, it was much more small in size. Albertosaurus dinosaurs are thought to have weighed less than 2 ton and to have grown to around 30 feet. The tyrannosaurus could weigh around 7 ton and could grow to just over 40 feet.

1    The word *feet* is a unit of measure. The word *feet* can also refer to part of the body. Complete the table below by listing the word that has both meanings.

| Word | Meaning 1 | Meaning 2 |
|------|-----------|-----------|
| feet | a unit measuring length | parts of the body at the end of the leg |
|      | a unit measuring length | the outdoor area around a house |
|      | a unit measuring weight | to hit something hard |
|      | a unit measuring length | to slowly move forward |

**2**   Which of these is the best way to rewrite the sentence below?

**However, it was much more small in size.**

Ⓐ   However, it was much smaller in size.

Ⓑ   However, it was more small in size.

Ⓒ   However, it was more smaller in size.

Ⓓ   However, it was much small in size.

**3**   Which of these is the correct way to punctuate the date in paragraph 1?

Ⓐ   June, 9 1884

Ⓑ   June 9, 1884

Ⓒ   June, 9, 1884

Ⓓ   It is correct as it is.

**4**   What is the correct way to spell *simalar*?

Ⓐ   similar

Ⓑ   simmalar

Ⓒ   simmilar

Ⓓ   simillar

**5**   Which of these shows the correct way to capitalize "north america"?

Ⓐ   north america

Ⓑ   North america

Ⓒ   north America

Ⓓ   North America

# Revising and Editing Quizzes

# Set 2

---

## Instructions

Read each passage. Each passage is followed by questions.

For each multiple-choice question, read the question carefully. Then select the best answer. Fill in the circle for the correct answer.

For other types of questions, follow the instructions given.

---

## Building Your Vocabulary

As you read the passages, list any words you do not understand below. Use a dictionary to look up the meaning of the word. Write the meaning of the word below.

Word: _____

Meaning: _____

_____

Word: _____

Meaning: _____

_____

Word: _____

Meaning: _____

_____

Word: _____

Meaning: _____

_____

Word: _____

Meaning: _____

_____

# Quiz 6

**Read the passage below. Then answer the questions that follow it.**

## Not a Farmer's Day

(1) It was a sunny afternoon in outback Springwater. (2) Noah a run-down farmer was slumped over on a bale of hay in his barn having a nap. (3) Then, a loud crash woke him from his slumber. (4) What is it now? Noah grumbled.

(5) He let out a huff and started storming toward the barn door. (6) Stepping outside, he furrowed his brow as the sun struck his weathered face. (7) Slowly, his sleepy eyes began to focus. (8) Noah gasped as he saw what all the fuss was about. (9) Noah must have been so tired he forgot to put the brakes on his tractor properly. (10) It had over the top of his brand new chicken coop rolled right over. (11) He sighed as he realized that he was only tired because he had spent the whole weekend working tirelessly on the chicken coop.

1    The author chooses words and phrases to help show how Noah feels. Answer the questions below about the author's word choices.

What does the phrase "slumped over" suggest about how Noah feels?

_____

_____

What does the phrase "storming toward" suggest about how Noah feels?

_____

_____

**2** Which of these shows a better transition word to use in sentence 3 to suggest that the sound was not expected?

    Ⓐ     Finally, a loud crash woke him from his slumber.

    Ⓑ     Suddenly, a loud crash woke him from his slumber.

    Ⓒ     Luckily, a loud crash woke him from his slumber.

    Ⓓ     Instead, a loud crash woke him from his slumber.

**3** Which of these shows the correct way to punctuate sentence 4?

    Ⓐ     "What is it now"? Noah grumbled.

    Ⓑ     "What is it now?" Noah grumbled.

    Ⓒ     "What is it now? Noah grumbled."

    Ⓓ     "What is it now? Noah grumbled".

**4** Which of these is the best way to rewrite sentence 10?

    Ⓐ     It had, right over the top of his brand new chicken coop, rolled.

    Ⓑ     His brand new chicken coop, rolled right over the top of it had.

    Ⓒ     His brand new chicken coop, it had rolled right over the top of.

    Ⓓ     It had rolled right over the top of his brand new chicken coop.

**5** Which of these shows the correct way to use commas in sentence 2?

    Ⓐ     Noah a run-down farmer, was slumped over on a bale of hay in his barn, having a nap.

    Ⓑ     Noah a run-down farmer was slumped over, on a bale of hay, in his barn having a nap.

    Ⓒ     Noah, a run-down farmer, was slumped over on a bale of hay in his barn having a nap.

    Ⓓ     Noah, a run-down farmer was slumped over on a bale of hay, in his barn having a nap.

## Quiz 7

**Read the passage below. Then answer the questions that follow it.**

### Many Moons

Saturn have many different and diverse moons. They range from moonlets less than a mile across to the enormous moon known as Titan. Titan is actually larger than the planet Mercury. It is even larger than the Earth's moon. In fact, it is allmost half the size of Earth.

In total, amongst all the debris that makes up Saturn's ring, Saturn has a staggering 62 moons. Of these, 53 have been given names. Most of the major moons are named after mythological figures associated with the Roman god of agriculture, Saturn.

### Saturn's Five Largest Moons

| Name | Diameter (kilometers) |
|---|---|
| Titan | 5,150 |
| Rhea | 1,527 |
| Lapetus | 1,470 |
| Dione | 1,123 |
| Enceladus | 504 |

1    The word *agriculture* contains the Latin root *agri-*. What does the Latin root *agri-* mean?

Ⓐ    water

Ⓑ    space

Ⓒ    field

Ⓓ    bird

**2**    Which change should be made in the sentence below?

**In fact, it is allmost half the size of Earth.**

Ⓐ    Delete the comma

Ⓑ    Change *allmost* to *almost*

Ⓒ    Change *half* to *halves*

Ⓓ    There is no change needed.

**3**    Which word should replace the word *have* in the first sentence?

Ⓐ    is

Ⓑ    has

Ⓒ    was

Ⓓ    were

**4**    Why does the author use the word *staggering* to describe Saturn's moons?

Ⓐ    to emphasize how many there are

Ⓑ    to suggest that they will not last

Ⓒ    to describe how they move

Ⓓ    to show that each one is different

**5**    Which meaning of the word *figures* is used in the last sentence?

Ⓐ    numbers

Ⓑ    diagrams

Ⓒ    totals or sums

Ⓓ    people or characters

# Quiz 8

**Read the passage below. Then answer the questions that follow it.**

## Dreams of Gold

Saturday had always been the day Marcy went to swimming class. Ever since she was six years old, Marcy and her mother had gone to the local swim center to practice with Coach Tyler and all of the other children from her neighborhood. Marcy loved swimming and had always been faster than everybody else in her class. Almost every night, Marcy dreamed about winning a gold medal at the state swimming competition.

Then girl called Morgan joined the class. Morgan swimmed faster than anyone Marcy had ever seen. Her legs kicked at a rappid pace. Her arms were a blur of movement. Suddenly, Marcy wasn't the fastest swimmer anymore.

Marcy decided she was not going to let anything stand in her way. She just started training harder. She worked so hard that she was able to beat Morgan. Marcy was proud of herself.

1      Read the sentence below.

**Marcy decided she was not going to let anything stand in her way.**

Explain the meaning of the phrase "not going to let anything stand in her way."

_____

_____

_____

**2** Which word should replace the word *swimmed* in the sentence below?

**Morgan swimmed faster than anyone Marcy had ever seen.**

Ⓐ      swim

Ⓑ      swam

Ⓒ      swimmer

Ⓓ      swimming

**3** Which change should be made in the sentence below?

**Her legs kicked at a rappid pace.**

Ⓐ      Change *legs* to *leg's*

Ⓑ      Change *rappid* to *rapid*

Ⓒ      Change *pace* to *pase*

Ⓓ      There is no change needed.

**4** What is the best way to rewrite the sentence below?

**Then girl called Morgan joined the class.**

Ⓐ      Then a girl called Morgan joined the class.

Ⓑ      Then the girl called Morgan joined the class.

Ⓒ      Then some girl called Morgan joined the class.

Ⓓ      Then this girl called Morgan joined the class.

# Quiz 9

**Read the passage below. Then answer the questions that follow it.**

## Musical Tastes

February 22 2012

Dear aunt brenda,

Today after school, I went over to Megan's house. We finished our homework, and then we talked about school and music! Megan is really into those really loud bands that seem to scream all the words. I just don't get it! Why listen to music if you can't even understand the words? Give me something I can sing to any day! Megan wanted me to listen to some songs. She turned on her CD player really loud. Suddenly it was like the room was filled with screaming monkeys! I listened to a few songs and really tried to enjoy it, but it just wasn't my thing. I guess we'll have to agree to disagree about music.

Bye for now,

Holly

1    In the passage, the author uses contractions. A contraction is a shortened form of two words. Write the long form of each of the contractions below.

don't          _____

can't          _____

wasn't         _____

we'll          _____

**2**  What does the prefix in the word *disagree* mean?

&#9398;  more

&#9399;  less

&#9400;  after

&#9401;  not

**3**  Which sentence should NOT end with an exclamation mark?

&#9398;  *We finished our homework, and then we talked about school and music!*

&#9399;  *I just don't get it!*

&#9400;  *Give me something I can sing to any day!*

&#9401;  *Suddenly it was like the room was filled with screaming monkeys!*

**4**  What is the correct way to start the letter?

&#9398;  Dear aunt Brenda,

&#9399;  Dear Aunt Brenda,

&#9400;  Dear aunt Brenda.

&#9401;  Dear Aunt Brenda.

**5**  What is the correct way to write the date at the start of the letter?

&#9398;  February, 22 2012

&#9399;  February 22, 2012

&#9400;  February, 22, 2012

&#9401;  It is correct as is.

# Quiz 10

**Read the passage below. Then answer the questions that follow it.**

**Chess**

Chess is a board game. It is played between two players on a checkerboard. Each player has sixteen pieces. The goal is to use your pieces to trap or "checkmate" the king. A "checkmate" occurs when the king cannot move without being taken by other piece.

There are different rules for how each chess piece can move. For example, a rook can only move up or down, while a bishop can only move diagonally. The king can move in any direction, but can only move one space. While it might seem simple, chess is a complex game. It takes a lot of strategy to win.

Chess is thought to have originated in India or China. It is one of the oldest board games in existence, alongside checkers and backgammon. During the 16th century, it became popular as a competitive board game. The game has continued to grow since then. The first official World Chess Champion was Wilhelm Steinitz, which claimed the title in 1886.

1    Which word should replace the word *other* in the sentence below?

> **A "checkmate" occurs when the king cannot move without being taken by other piece.**

Ⓐ    different

Ⓑ    another

Ⓒ    anyone

Ⓓ    more

**2**  Which of these shows the best way to rewrite the second sentence?

Ⓐ   It is on a checkerboard played between two players.

Ⓑ   Between two players it is played on a checkerboard.

Ⓒ   Between two players on a checkerboard it is played.

Ⓓ   It is played on a checkerboard between two players.

**3**  The word *originated* contains the base word *origin*. What does the word *originated* most likely mean?

Ⓐ   forgotten

Ⓑ   started

Ⓒ   changed

Ⓓ   studied

**4**  In the sentence below, the word *grow* refers to an increase in what?

**The game has continued to grow since then.**

Ⓐ   how difficult chess is

Ⓑ   how large the chess board is

Ⓒ   how popular chess is

Ⓓ   how long a chess game takes

**5**  Which word should replace the word *which* in the last sentence?

Ⓐ   that

Ⓑ   who

Ⓒ   him

Ⓓ   he

# Revising and Editing Quizzes

# Set 3

---

**Instructions**

Read each passage. Each passage is followed by questions.

For each multiple-choice question, read the question carefully. Then select the best answer. Fill in the circle for the correct answer.

For other types of questions, follow the instructions given.

---

# Building Your Vocabulary

As you read the passages, list any words you do not understand below. Use a dictionary to look up the meaning of the word. Write the meaning of the word below.

Word: _____

Meaning: _____

_____

Word: _____

Meaning: _____

_____

Word: _____

Meaning: _____

_____

Word: _____

Meaning: _____

_____

Word: _____

Meaning: _____

_____

# Quiz 11

**Read the passage below. Then answer the questions that follow it.**

## Missing a Frend

Lying underneath a star-sprinkled sky.
Here I sit just wondering why.
It was on this day, years ago, we met.
I miss you now, my dear faithful pet.

1    Alliteration is the repetition of consonant sounds in neighboring words. For example, the phrase "good as gold" uses alliteration because of the repeated *g* sound. Identify the two examples of alliteration in the poem. Write the words on the lines below. Then write two more examples of your own.

Example from the poem:

_____

Example from the poem:

_____

Own example:

_____

Own example:

_____

**2**    Which line from the poem is NOT a complete sentence?

Ⓐ    Line 1

Ⓑ    Line 2

Ⓒ    Line 3

Ⓓ    Line 4

**3**    Which word in the second line is a pronoun?

Ⓐ    I

Ⓑ    sit

Ⓒ    wondering

Ⓓ    why

**4**    What is the correct way to spell *frend*?

Ⓐ    freind

Ⓑ    friend

Ⓒ    frened

Ⓓ    frenned

**5**    Which meaning of the word *dear* is most likely used in the last line?

Ⓐ    costly

Ⓑ    darling

Ⓒ    rare

Ⓓ    serious

# Quiz 12

**Read the passage below. Then answer the questions that follow it.**

## The New Boy

Lionel sat and stared at his mother in the kitchen. "But why would I want to do that?" he asked with a befuddled look.

His mother chuckled quietly and smiled. Lionel had just finished telling his mother that a new kid had started at the school that day. He had explained that the boy dressed strangely. He had explained that the boy had a weird haircut. He had explained that the boy didn't seem to fit in with anyone. His mother had suggested that he should make friends with that boy.

"You should make an effort to being friends with everybody," his mother said. "After all, what if that other boy was you?"

Lionel sat and thought about it for a while. The more he thought about it, the more he realized that it would mean a lot to him if someone tried to make friends with him, or at least talked to him. He decided that his mother had a good point.

1    Which word or words should replace *being* in the sentence below?

   **"You should make an effort to being friends with everybody," his mother said.**

   Ⓐ    be

   Ⓑ    been

   Ⓒ    will be

   Ⓓ    have been

**2**   In the last sentence, the phrase "had a good point" means that the mother was –

   Ⓐ     wrong

   Ⓑ     right

   Ⓒ     proud

   Ⓓ     angry

**3**   What does the word *strangely* mean?

   Ⓐ     in a way that is strange

   Ⓑ     the most strange

   Ⓒ     someone who is strange

   Ⓓ     more strange

**4**   Which of these shows the best way to combine the sentences below?

> **He had explained that the boy dressed strangely. He had explained that the boy had a weird haircut. He had explained that the boy didn't seem to fit in with anyone.**

   Ⓐ     He had explained that the boy dressed strangely, weird haircut, didn't seem to fit in with anyone.

   Ⓑ     He had explained that the boy dressed strangely, weird haircut, and didn't seem to fit in with anyone.

   Ⓒ     He had explained that the boy dressed strangely, had a weird haircut, didn't seem to fit in with anyone.

   Ⓓ     He had explained that the boy dressed strangely, had a weird haircut, and didn't seem to fit in with anyone.

# Quiz 13

**Read the passage below. Then answer the questions that follow it.**

## Anne Frank

(1) Anne Frank was a teenage girl who was given a diary for her thirteen birthday. (2) Anne used the diary to record the events she lived through during World War II. (3) The diary describes her life from June 1942 until August 1944. (4) During this time, Anne Frank and her family were living in hiding. (5) The diary is a moving account of life during World War II. (6) Despite the difficulty of Anne Frank's life, the diary is generally positive and uplifting.

(7) The diary eventually found its way to a publisher in Amsterdam. (8) The first edition of *The diary of a young girl* was printed in 1947. (9) It has since become one of the most widely read books in the world. (10) It has been published in over 60 languages from all around the world. (11) It has been read by over 10 million people worldwide. (12) Many people still enjoy reading Anne Frank's famous book. (13) She is admired for her honesty. (14) She is also admired for writing about a difficult time without losing hope.

1    Where would be the best place to add the sentence below?

**The book has been made into plays and films.**

Ⓐ    After sentence 2

Ⓑ    After sentence 6

Ⓒ    After sentence 11

Ⓓ    After sentence 14

**2**   Which of these is the correct way to capitalize the title of Anne Frank's book?

    Ⓐ   *The Diary of a young Girl*

    Ⓑ   *The Diary of a Young Girl*

    Ⓒ   *The Diary Of a Young Girl*

    Ⓓ   *The Diary Of A Young Girl*

**3**   Which change should be made in sentence 1?

    Ⓐ   Change *teenage* to *teenager*

    Ⓑ   Change *thirteen* to *thirteenth*

    Ⓒ   Change *birthday* to *Birthday*

    Ⓓ   There is no change needed.

**4**   Which of these shows the best way to shorten sentence 10 without changing its meaning?

    Ⓐ   It has been published all around the world.

    Ⓑ   It has been published in over 60 languages.

    Ⓒ   It has been published in languages from all around the world.

    Ⓓ   It has been in over 60 languages from all around the world.

**5**   Which sentence would be best to add to the beginning of the passage to state the central idea?

    Ⓐ   Everyone should think about keeping a diary.

    Ⓑ   Some teenagers have many problems to face.

    Ⓒ   You should never secretly read another person's diary.

    Ⓓ   Anne Frank wrote an important book that is still read today.

# Quiz 14

**Read the passage below. Then answer the questions that follow it.**

## Mindful of Monsters

When you are alone at night, do you ever think about monsters? Do you wonder if there are any lurking under your bed? Maybe you think they could be hiding in the closet? Could they be hiding behind the door?

Or maybe you don't think about monsters at all. Perhaps you think the possibility is ridiculous. After all, everyone knows that monsters do not exist. Well, that is what I would want you to think if I were a monster.

I guess you never bother to check under your bed, in your closet, or behind all those closed doors anymore. Maybe there is a monster lurking somewhere you no longer look not anymore. Maybe it's time to check. Or, if the monster has never bothered you before, maybe you just leave him alone to hide quietly in his home.

1    The author uses the word *lurking* in the first and last paragraphs. Explain why the author uses the word *lurking*. Think about what the word means and what it suggests about the monster.

_____

_____

_____

_____

_____

**2**  Which sentence from the first paragraph should NOT end with a question mark?

    Ⓐ      *When you are alone at night, do you ever think about monsters?*

    Ⓑ      *Do you wonder if there are any lurking under your bed?*

    Ⓒ      *Maybe you think they could be hiding in the closet?*

    Ⓓ      *Could they be hiding behind the door?*


**3**  What does the word *ridiculous* mean in the second paragraph?

    Ⓐ      scary

    Ⓑ      likely

    Ⓒ      silly

    Ⓓ      possible


**4**  Which change should be made in the sentence below?

> **Maybe there is a monster lurking somewhere you no longer look not anymore.**

    Ⓐ      Change *there* to *their*

    Ⓑ      Change *somewhere* to *some where*

    Ⓒ      Change *you* to *your*

    Ⓓ      Delete the words *not anymore*


**5**  Which change should be made in the last sentence?

    Ⓐ      Change *bothered* to *botherred*

    Ⓑ      Change *leave* to *left*

    Ⓒ      Change *quietly* to *quietness*

    Ⓓ      There is no change needed.

## Quiz 15

**Read the passage below. Then answer the questions that follow it.**

### Peace

Did you know that the peace symbol was originally created to protest against the use of nuclear weapons? It was designed by Gerald Holtom in 1958. He was a designer and graduate of London's Royal College of Arts.

Semaphore is a system of signaling that involves waving a pair of flags in a certain pattern. Each pattern represents a letter of the alphabet. Holtom based his design on this system. He used the semaphore letters for N and D to form the symbol. He chose those letters because they standed for nuclear disarmament. Holtoms design went on to become known worldwide as a general symbol for peace.

**Symbol for N**      **Symbol for D**      **Peace Symbol**

1     The passage uses the word *peace*. The word *piece* sounds the same as *peace*, but has a different meaning. Write the meaning of the word *piece* below. Then write a sentence using the word.

Meaning:

_____

Sentence:

_____

_____

**2** Based on the suffix, what is the meaning of the word *designer*?

Ⓐ     someone who designs

Ⓑ     used to design

Ⓒ     to become a design

Ⓓ     full of design

**3** Which word from the passage begins with a silent letter?

Ⓐ     system

Ⓑ     waving

Ⓒ     design

Ⓓ     known

**4** Which word or words should replace *standed* in the sentence below?

**He chose those letters because they standed for nuclear disarmament.**

Ⓐ     stood

Ⓑ     did stand

Ⓒ     have stood

Ⓓ     standing

**5** Which change should be made in the last sentence?

Ⓐ     Change *Holtoms* to *Holtom's*

Ⓑ     Change *general* to *jeneral*

Ⓒ     Change *for* to *about*

Ⓓ     There is no change needed.

# Revising and Editing Quizzes

# Set 4

---

## Instructions

Read each passage. Each passage is followed by questions.

For each multiple-choice question, read the question carefully. Then select the best answer. Fill in the circle for the correct answer.

For other types of questions, follow the instructions given.

---

# Building Your Vocabulary

As you read the passages, list any words you do not understand below. Use a dictionary to look up the meaning of the word. Write the meaning of the word below.

Word: _____

Meaning: _____

_____

Word: _____

Meaning: _____

_____

Word: _____

Meaning: _____

_____

Word: _____

Meaning: _____

_____

Word: _____

Meaning: _____

_____

## Quiz 16

**Read the passage below. Then answer the questions that follow it.**

### Occam's Razor

Occam's razor is a scientific principle that can be applied to many areas of science. It was developed by William of Ochkam in the 14th century. William of Ochkam was a philosopher born in the english county of Surrey.

Occam's razor explains that if you have a number of competing theories, the simplest theory is most likely to be correct. This is sometimes stated as the idea that the simplest answer is often the right one. Occam's razor is commonly applied in a number of scientific fields. These range from physics to medicine.

Occam's razor can also be used in everyday life. Now imagine that your school bus does not turn up on time one morning. Why not! One theory is that all the street signs were stolen the night before, so the bus driver is lost. Another theory is that the bus is stuck in traffic. Which theory do you think is probably correct?

1     The word *physics* starts with the letters *ph*, but these letters make an "f" sound. Complete each sentence below by adding a word that starts with the letters *ph* or *f*.

      We used the camera to take a _____.

      A square has _____ sides.

      There were six pigs and eight goats on the _____.

      I used my cell _____ to call my mother.

      I listened to the load croaking of the _____.

      The parrot had bright green _____.

**2**   Which word from the passage should start with a capital letter?

Ⓐ   principle

Ⓑ   century

Ⓒ   english

Ⓓ   prediction

**3**   Which meaning of the word *fields* is used in the sentence below?

**Occam's razor is commonly applied in a number of scientific fields.**

Ⓐ   meadows or farmlands

Ⓑ   sports grounds

Ⓒ   subjects or areas

Ⓓ   deals with

**4**   What is the meaning of the word *simplest*?

Ⓐ   more simple

Ⓑ   the most simple

Ⓒ   to make simpler

Ⓓ   in a simple way

**5**   Which change should be made in the last paragraph?

Ⓐ   Change *imagine* to *imajine*

Ⓑ   Change *night* to *knight*

Ⓒ   Change *Why not!* to *Why not?*

Ⓓ   There is no change needed.

# Quiz 17

**Read the passage below. Then answer the questions that follow it.**

## The Ambassadors

The oil painting titled *The Ambassadors* was created by Hans Holbein the Younger in 1533. Hans Holbein the Younger was a German artist best known for painting portraits. The painting are a portrait of two people. It also contains a number of items that have been drawn in a careful way. It has been the subject of much discussion through art studies and literature.

*The Ambassadors* is most famous for the introduction of anamorphic design into hand-painted art. Anamorphic design refers to design where images can only be seen from a certain angle. At the bottom of *The Ambassadors*, a skewed object can be seen. From front on, you cannot tell what the object is. If you are viewing the painting from the side, the same object is easily recognizeable as a skull. The painting can be viewed in Great Britain's National Gallery, that is located in London. While the painting may not immediately seem interesting, it is certainly worth a second look.

1    Which word should replace the word *that* in the sentence below?

> **The painting can be viewed in Great Britain's National Gallery, that is located in London.**

    Ⓐ    who

    Ⓑ    where

    Ⓒ    which

    Ⓓ    whom

**2**  Which word from the passage has the same beginning sound as *search*?

Ⓐ  created

Ⓑ  contains

Ⓒ  careful

Ⓓ  certain

**3**  What is the best way to rewrite the end of the sentence below?

**It also contains a number of items that have been drawn in a careful way.**

Ⓐ  It also contains a number of careful drawn items.

Ⓑ  It also contains a number of drawn careful items.

Ⓒ  It also contains a number of carefully drawn items.

Ⓓ  It also contains a number of drawn carefully items.

**4**  Which change should be made in the sentence below?

**The painting are a portrait of two people.**

Ⓐ  Change *are* to *is*

Ⓑ  Delete the word *a*

Ⓒ  Change *two* to *too*

Ⓓ  Change *people* to *peoples*

**5**  Which of these is the correct way to spell *recognizeable*?

Ⓐ  recognizible

Ⓑ  recognizable

Ⓒ  recognizzable

Ⓓ  recognizzeable

# Quiz 18

**Read the passage below. Then answer the questions that follow it.**

## The Old Hollow Bakery

Peering through the window at Old Hollow Bakery, you could see a selection of fine treats. There would be wonderful brownies, mouth-watering cakes, and fresh cookies. There would be boxes of donuts and a large assortment of other goodies. There would also be hundreds of fresh loaves of bread.

It was all in a day's work for Ms. Dunn, the baker from Old Hollow. Ms. Dunn loved opening her shop in the morning. All the town's children would rush in on their way to school and pick themselves up some tastey treats.

Ms. Dunn so early getting up didn't even mind. When she got up, the sun hadn't even peeked its head above the horizon. As she baked, the sun slowly rose. Finally, it was time for the children to arrive. They rushed in to see what treats she had made for them. Just one smile made Ms. Dunn feel like all the hard work was worth it.

1   The plural of *cake* is made by adding *s*. The plural of *box* is made by adding *es*. The plural of *loaf* has a special form. The word *loaves* is the plural form of *loaf*. Write the plural form of each word below.

bike   _____          man   _____

mouse _____          fox    _____

shell  _____          leaf   _____

dress  _____          eagle  _____

beach  _____          knife  _____

**2** What is the abbreviation *Ms.* short for?

&#9398; Miss

&#9399; Missus

&#9400; Master

&#9401; Madams

**3** Which word could replace the word *rushed* in the sentence below without changing the meaning of the sentence?

**They rushed in to see what treats she had made for them.**

&#9398; wandered

&#9399; hurried

&#9400; stomped

&#9401; strolled

**4** Which change should be made in the second paragraph?

&#9398; Change *day's* to *days*

&#9399; Change *children* to *childs*

&#9400; Change *their* to *they're*

&#9401; Change *tastey* to *tasty*

**5** What is the best way to rewrite the first sentence of paragraph 3?

&#9398; Ms. Dunn so early didn't even mind getting up.

&#9399; Ms. Dunn getting up didn't even mind so early.

&#9400; Ms. Dunn didn't even mind getting up so early.

&#9401; Ms. Dunn didn't even mind so early getting up.

## Quiz 19

**Read the passage below. Then answer the questions that follow it.**

### going to a show

It was summer vacation. For Jacob, that meant going home to Chicago. He wouldn't usually be so excited about it, but this time was different. This summer, he was going to be seeing Dodger in concert.

Jacob had won a free ticket to see his favorite band after uploading a video of him singing one of their songs to an online contest. Seeing Dodger would be something Jacob would never forgotten.

The biggest problem he'd had was trying to choose just three friends to take with him. He wished that all his friends could go. He had finally choosed the three friends that he knew adored Dodger just as much as he did. He felt sad about not taking his best friend Andrew, but he knew that Andrew didn't like Dodger's music that much. Jacob's friends were all overjoyed when he told them the good news. Now the concert was just a week away and Jacob could hardly wait.

1    Divide the following words from the passage into two syllables. The first one has been completed for you.

summer    _____sum / mer_____          biggest    _____

concert    _____          problem    _____

ticket    _____          adored    _____

contest    _____          music    _____

**2**  Which word should replace *forgotten* in the sentence below?

**Seeing Dodger would be something Jacob would never forgotten.**

Ⓐ     forgot

Ⓑ     forget

Ⓒ     forgets

Ⓓ     forgetful

**3**  What is the correct way to capitalize the title of the passage?

Ⓐ     Going to a show

Ⓑ     Going To a Show

Ⓒ     Going to a Show

Ⓓ     Going To A Show

**4**  Which word should replace *choosed* in paragraph 3?

Ⓐ     chosed

Ⓑ     chosen

Ⓒ     choose

Ⓓ     choosen

**5**  Which word is a synonym for *overjoyed*?

Ⓐ     upset

Ⓑ     shocked

Ⓒ     proud

Ⓓ     delighted

## Quiz 20

**Read the passage below. Then answer the questions that follow it.**

## Computer Health

Many of us receive vaccinations and booster shots from time to time to keep us healthy and help stop the spread of viruses. Computers are much the same! We should all make sure a quality antivirus program is installed and updated frequently on our home computers. How should we do this?

Step 1: Research what antivirus software you think would be best to use.

Step 2: Install the software onto your computer.

Step 3: Run a scan of your computer to make sure your drive is free from viruses.

Step 4: Keep updating the software often to make sure it can spot new viruses.

---

**TIP**

New viruses are being created all the time. A virus program can only fight the viruses it knows about. That's why it is important to update your virus program often. Every time you update the software, it will be told about new viruses. It is a good idea to set a day each week to check that your software is up-to-date.

---

1    In the passage, the word *spot* means "see or notice." The word *spot* can also have other meanings. Write a definition of another meaning for *spot* below. Then write a sentence that uses the word.

Definition: _____

Sentence: _____

**2** What does the prefix in the word *antivirus* mean?

Ⓐ     before

Ⓑ     against

Ⓒ     after

Ⓓ     more

**3** Which phrase has the same meaning as "from time to time"?

Ⓐ     hardly every

Ⓑ     twice a year

Ⓒ     every now and then

Ⓓ     over and over again

**4** Where would be the best place to add the following step?

**Buy the software you have selected.**

Ⓐ     Before Step 1

Ⓑ     After Step 1

Ⓒ     After Step 3

Ⓓ     After Step 4

**5** Which sentence could best be added to the start of the first paragraph to state the main idea?

Ⓐ     Computers have made life much easier.

Ⓑ     Just like you, computers need to be looked after.

Ⓒ     There are several different types of computers.

Ⓓ     Many people find it hard to imagine life without computers.

# Section 2
# Language, Vocabulary, and Grammar
# Quizzes

---

### Instructions

For each multiple-choice question, read the question carefully. Then select the best answer. Fill in the circle for the correct answer.

For other types of questions, follow the instructions given.

---

## Quiz 21: Analyze Words

1    The word *bring* ends in *ing*. Which letters can NOT be added to the beginning of *ing* to form another word?

Ⓐ    sh

Ⓑ    sw

Ⓒ    st

Ⓓ    str


2    In which word does *oo* sound the same as in *cook*?

Ⓐ    spoon

Ⓑ    room

Ⓒ    foot

Ⓓ    loop


3    Which word rhymes with *white*?

Ⓐ    straight

Ⓑ    wait

Ⓒ    light

Ⓓ    wise


4    Which word does NOT rhyme with the three other words?

Ⓐ    where

Ⓑ    square

Ⓒ    here

Ⓓ    their

## Quiz 22: Identify and Use Antonyms

**Antonyms are words that have opposite meanings. Use antonyms to fill in the blank spaces.**

1    man: woman            boy: _____

2    big: small            huge: _____

3    happy: sad            laugh: _____

4    day: night            awake: _____

5    The rock was hard. The pillow was _____.

6    The fastest runner came first. The slowest runner came_____.

7    I threw out the old dress. I bought a _____ dress.

8    It is warm outside. It is cool _____.

9    The pool is shallow at one end, but _____ at the other end.

10   The room was messy. The room was _____ after I cleaned it.

## Quiz 23: Understand the Meaning of Idioms

**Idioms are phrases that have special meanings. The meaning is not based on the usual meanings of the words. For each sentence below, choose the correct meaning of the underlined idiom.**

**1**    The test was <u>a piece of cake</u>.

    Ⓐ    very easy

    Ⓑ    very hard

    Ⓒ    very short

    Ⓓ    very long

**2**    Sam was <u>on the fence</u> about going to the party.

    Ⓐ    excited

    Ⓑ    worried

    Ⓒ    undecided

    Ⓓ    certain

**3**    The new diner was <u>all the rage</u>.

    Ⓐ    costly

    Ⓑ    empty

    Ⓒ    pretty

    Ⓓ    popular

**4**    Julie and Patrice are <u>like day and night</u>.

    Ⓐ    great friends

    Ⓑ    very different

    Ⓒ    quite unusual

    Ⓓ    twin sisters

## Quiz 24: Use Modal Verbs Correctly

**For each sentence below, choose the word that best completes the sentence.**

1    After seeing the guard dog, Blake decided he _____ not enter.

    Ⓐ    shall

    Ⓑ    should

    Ⓒ    will

    Ⓓ    can

2    "I _____ buy that dress if I have enough money left," Mia said.

    Ⓐ    might

    Ⓑ    would

    Ⓒ    must

    Ⓓ    can

3    The drama teacher warned that we all _____ know our lines.

    Ⓐ    could

    Ⓑ    must

    Ⓒ    shall

    Ⓓ    can

4    "I have to go to the dentist, so _____ I leave class early today?" Bryan asked.

    Ⓐ    may

    Ⓑ    shall

    Ⓒ    will

    Ⓓ    would

## Quiz 25: Use Words with Suffixes

**For each question below, select the word that correctly completes the sentence.**

1    Amy's writing was so messy that is was only just _____.

    Ⓐ     reads

    Ⓑ     reading

    Ⓒ     readership

    Ⓓ     readable

2    Amanda _____ showed her mother her first place ribbon.

    Ⓐ     proudly

    Ⓑ     proudest

    Ⓒ     proudness

    Ⓓ     prouder

3    Hans found it easy to study in the library because of the _____.

    Ⓐ     quietly

    Ⓑ     quietness

    Ⓒ     quieter

    Ⓓ     quietest

4    The group wandered _____ through the desert.

    Ⓐ     aimless

    Ⓑ     aims

    Ⓒ     aimlessly

    Ⓓ     aimed

## Quiz 26: Spell Commonly Misspelled Words

**For each question below, circle the word in the sentence that is spelled incorrectly. Write the correct spelling of the word on the line.**

1    I was late to school this morning becuase my alarm clock failed.

_____

2    The children were told to sit still untill they were told they could leave.

_____

3    It was reelly cold early today, but it is much warmer now.

_____

4    Most people have a favrite movie, but I can never decide on just one.

_____

5    Corey's bedroom looked quite diffrent after he finished cleaning it.

_____

6    I have always wanted anuther younger sister.

_____

## Quiz 27: Understand and Use Prefixes

1    Based on the prefix, what is a *precooked* meal?

Ⓐ    a meal that is not cooked

Ⓑ    a meal that is easy to cook

Ⓒ    a meal that was cooked before

Ⓓ    a meal that is cooked once

2    Which prefix can be added to the word *match* to make a word meaning "not match"?

Ⓐ    un-

Ⓑ    re-

Ⓒ    mis-

Ⓓ    pre-

3    Which prefix should be added to the word to make the sentence correct?

**Simon turned off the power and __plugged his laptop.**

Ⓐ    un-

Ⓑ    dis-

Ⓒ    in-

Ⓓ    mis-

4    Which word contains the prefix *re-*?

Ⓐ    reason

Ⓑ    recharge

Ⓒ    regular

Ⓓ    result

## Quiz 28: Understand and Use Suffixes

**1**    What does the word *tasteless* mean?

    Ⓐ    had taste

    Ⓑ    without taste

    Ⓒ    more taste

    Ⓓ    the act of tasting

**2**    Which suffix can be added to the word *move* to make a word meaning "the act of moving"?

    Ⓐ    -able

    Ⓑ    -ed

    Ⓒ    -less

    Ⓓ    -ment

**3**    Which word makes the sentence correct?

**The bread had been_____ baked that morning.**

    Ⓐ    fresher

    Ⓑ    freshly

    Ⓒ    freshest

    Ⓓ    freshness

**4**    Which word means "the most calm"?

    Ⓐ    calmer

    Ⓑ    calmest

    Ⓒ    calmness

    Ⓓ    calming

# Quiz 29: Understand Greek and Latin Word Parts

1   The word *microscope* contains a Greek root meaning –

Ⓐ   large

Ⓑ   small

Ⓒ   fast

Ⓓ   slow

2   The word *audiology* contains the Latin root *audi-*. *Audiology* is probably the study of –

Ⓐ   hearing

Ⓑ   light

Ⓒ   birds

Ⓓ   water

3   A *centenary* is a period of one hundred years. A *bicentenary* is probably a period of how many years?

Ⓐ   two hundred

Ⓑ   three hundred

Ⓒ   four hundred

Ⓓ   five hundred

4   A *pentathlon* is a sports contest made up of several events. The word *pentathlon* contains the Greek root *penta-*. How many events does a *pentathlon* most likely have?

Ⓐ   4

Ⓑ   5

Ⓒ   8

Ⓓ   10

# Quiz 30: Spell Words with Suffixes Correctly

**1**   Which word is spelled incorrectly?

Ⓐ   screaming

Ⓑ   shoutting

Ⓒ   yelling

Ⓓ   crying


**2**   Which underlined word is spelled incorrectly?

Ⓐ   <u>playful</u> child

Ⓑ   <u>slippery</u> floor

Ⓒ   <u>dangerous</u> storm

Ⓓ   <u>upseting</u> news


**3**   Which word is spelled incorrectly?

Ⓐ   awfuly

Ⓑ   marching

Ⓒ   powerful

Ⓓ   priceless


**4**   Which underlined word is spelled incorrectly?

Ⓐ   coin <u>collection</u>

Ⓑ   fun <u>celebrashon</u>

Ⓒ   sad <u>disappointment</u>

Ⓓ   great <u>improvement</u>

## Quiz 31: Use Contractions

**A contraction is a shortened form of two words. For example, *I am* can be shortened to *I'm*. For each question below, write the contraction for the two words given. Then write a sentence that uses the contraction.**

**1**    he has    _____

_____

**2**    I will    _____

_____

**3**    that would    _____

_____

**4**    where is    _____

_____

**5**    we are    _____

_____

**6**    should not    _____

_____

## Quiz 32: Use Prepositions

**For each question below, select the word that best completes the sentence.**

1    I put socks _____ my feet to warm them up.

    Ⓐ    out

    Ⓑ    on

    Ⓒ    next

    Ⓓ    to

2    The teacher took her seat _____ her desk.

    Ⓐ    after

    Ⓑ    between

    Ⓒ    behind

    Ⓓ    onto

3    We had apple pie _____ dinner.

    Ⓐ    beyond

    Ⓑ    about

    Ⓒ    beside

    Ⓓ    after

4    I usually walk to school _____ my two brothers.

    Ⓐ    with

    Ⓑ    for

    Ⓒ    from

    Ⓓ    at

## Quiz 33: Identify Proper Nouns

**Proper nouns start with a capital letter. For each question below, identify the proper nouns in the sentence. Then rewrite the sentence with the proper nouns capitalized.**

1      Miss williams taught us about the cold war.

_____

2      The rocky mountains are in north america.

_____

3      My friend amanda can speak spanish.

_____

4      My cousin charlie lives in alaska.

_____

5      It can get really hot during june and july.

_____

6      My mother is french, but she grew up in miami.

_____

## Quiz 34: Use Verbs Correctly

**1**    Which word or phrase makes the sentence complete?

**We _____ out at the lovely view.**

Ⓐ    looks

Ⓑ    looked

Ⓒ    looking

Ⓓ    is looking

**2**    Which word or phrase makes the sentence complete?

**I always _____ my teeth before I go to bed each night.**

Ⓐ    brush

Ⓑ    brushes

Ⓒ    was brushing

Ⓓ    have brushed

**3**    Which words make the sentence complete?

**Karen _____ on her bed, when she fell off and hurt her ankle.**

Ⓐ    has jumped

Ⓑ    will jump

Ⓒ    was jumping

Ⓓ    will have jumped

## Quiz 35: Use Correct Verb Tense

**For each question below, choose the correct verb tense to complete the sentence.**

1   I _____ too much cake at the party yesterday.

   Ⓐ   eat

   Ⓑ   ate

   Ⓒ   eaten

   Ⓓ   eated

2   The bus was late, so we had to _____ a long time.

   Ⓐ   waited

   Ⓑ   wait

   Ⓒ   waiting

   Ⓓ   will wait

3   Juan _____ his dog for a walk even if it is raining.

   Ⓐ   took

   Ⓑ   was taking

   Ⓒ   will take

   Ⓓ   has taken

4   Next week, I _____ to school from my grandmother's house.

   Ⓐ   was walking

   Ⓑ   has walked

   Ⓒ   have walked

   Ⓓ   will walk

## Quiz 36: Use Correct Subject-Verb Agreement

**For each question below, choose the word that best completes the sentence.**

1      We _____ hoping to come first, but we came second.

    Ⓐ    was

    Ⓑ    were

    Ⓒ    is

    Ⓓ    are

2      The elephant _____ water on its skin every morning.

    Ⓐ    spray

    Ⓑ    sprays

    Ⓒ    spraying

    Ⓓ    sprayer

3      Ryan and I _____ planning a camping trip for next weekend.

    Ⓐ    am

    Ⓑ    is

    Ⓒ    are

    Ⓓ    was

4      "There _____ to be a quicker way to get there," Jonah said.

    Ⓐ    are

    Ⓑ    were

    Ⓒ    has

    Ⓓ    have

## Quiz 37: Use Pronouns

**1**    Which sentence best combines the two sentences?

**Danny heated up the noodle soup.**
**Danny ate the noodle soup.**

Ⓐ    Danny heated up the noodle soup and ate him.

Ⓑ    Danny heated up the noodle soup and ate them.

Ⓒ    Danny heated up the noodle soup and ate it.

Ⓓ    Danny heated up the noodle soup and ate her.

**2**    Which sentence best combines the two sentences?

**Ty wrapped up the present for his sister.**
**Ty gave the present to his sister.**

Ⓐ    Ty wrapped up the present for his sister and gave it to him.

Ⓑ    Ty wrapped up the present for his sister and gave it to it.

Ⓒ    Ty wrapped up the present for his sister and gave it to her.

Ⓓ    Ty wrapped up the present for his sister and gave it to us.

**3**    Which sentence best combines the two sentences?

**Tia asked her brother for help.**
**Tia's brother agreed to help Tia.**

Ⓐ    Tia asked her brother for help, and he agreed to help she.

Ⓑ    Tia asked her brother for help, and him agreed to help she.

Ⓒ    Tia asked her brother for help, and he agreed to help her.

Ⓓ    Tia asked her brother for help, and him agreed to help her.

## Quiz 38: Use Adverbs

**Adverbs can describe how something is done. These adverbs often end in _ly_. Complete each sentence by adding an adverb ending in _ly_. The first one has been completed for you.**

**1**   I asked _nicely_ if I could get a lift to school.

**2**   I _____ raced home from school.

**3**   When I gave my speech, I tried to speak _____.

**4**   I was worried about falling, so I climbed the tree _____.

**5**   I spoke _____ so I would not wake up my sister.

**Adverbs can also describe how often something is done. For each sentence below, choose the adverb from the list that best completes the sentence.**

always        every        often        never        once

**6**   Great films should be watched at least _____.

**7**   Phil hates peas, so he _____ eats them.

**8**   I listen to music _____ afternoon.

**9**   You should _____ wear a seatbelt when in a car.

**10**   I _____ help my younger sister with her homework.

## Quiz 39: Spell Words Correctly

**1**   Which underlined word is spelled incorrectly?

   Ⓐ    <u>delivery</u> driver

   Ⓑ    to pay <u>attension</u>

   Ⓒ    traffic <u>accident</u>

   Ⓓ    <u>department</u> store


**2**   Which underlined word is spelled incorrectly?

   Ⓐ    simple <u>explanation</u>

   Ⓑ    a <u>dozen</u> eggs

   Ⓒ    <u>cotton</u> tablecloth

   Ⓓ    fashion <u>magezine</u>


**3**   Which underlined word is spelled incorrectly?

   Ⓐ    <u>handsome</u> man

   Ⓑ    <u>pumpkin</u> pie

   Ⓒ    <u>knives</u> and forks

   Ⓓ    <u>thum</u> and fingers


**4**   Which underlined word is spelled incorrectly?

   Ⓐ    take the <u>plunge</u>

   Ⓑ    boat and <u>paddel</u>

   Ⓒ    bite your <u>tongue</u>

   Ⓓ    solve a <u>riddle</u>

# Quiz 40: Choose Words or Phrases to Complete Sentences

**For each question below, choose the word or phrase that best completes the sentence.**

1   _____ you finish writing a story, you should check your spelling.

   Ⓐ   Earlier

   Ⓑ   After

   Ⓒ   Now

   Ⓓ   During

2   We woke up very early. It was _____ the sun was even up.

   Ⓐ   before

   Ⓑ   around

   Ⓒ   about

   Ⓓ   while

3   People should not send text messages _____ they are driving.

   Ⓐ   while

   Ⓑ   until

   Ⓒ   after

   Ⓓ   before

4   The hike seemed to take forever. _____, we reached the lookout.

   Ⓐ   From time to time

   Ⓑ   Quickly

   Ⓒ   To begin with

   Ⓓ   Finally

## Quiz 41: Use Context to Determine Word Meanings

1      What does the word *mistake* mean in the sentence below?

**Hunter felt bad because he knew he had made a mistake.**

Ⓐ      reason

Ⓑ      wrong

Ⓒ      problem

Ⓓ      error

2      What does the word *saved* mean in the sentence below?

**The hero saved the boy from falling off the bridge.**

Ⓐ      rescued

Ⓑ      pushed

Ⓒ      jumped

Ⓓ      brave

3      What does the word *tasty* mean in the sentence below?

**Grandma cooked tasty soup for lunch.**

Ⓐ      awful

Ⓑ      pasty

Ⓒ      delicious

Ⓓ      hot

## Quiz 42: Use Frequently Confused Words

**1**    In which sentence are the underlined words used correctly?

    Ⓐ    The soap had a lovely <u>sent</u> of apples and <u>pairs</u>.

    Ⓑ    The soap had a lovely <u>sent</u> of apples and <u>pears</u>.

    Ⓒ    The soap had a lovely <u>scent</u> of apples and <u>pairs</u>.

    Ⓓ    The soap had a lovely <u>scent</u> of apples and <u>pears</u>.


**2**    In which sentence are the underlined words used correctly?

    Ⓐ    There were <u>two</u> many players on the basketball <u>court</u>.

    Ⓑ    There were <u>two</u> many players on the basketball <u>caught</u>.

    Ⓒ    There were <u>too</u> many players on the basketball <u>court</u>.

    Ⓓ    There were <u>too</u> many players on the basketball <u>caught</u>.


**3**    In which sentence is the underlined word used correctly?

    Ⓐ    Samuel got almost all the questions <u>rite</u>.

    Ⓑ    Samuel got almost all the questions <u>write</u>.

    Ⓒ    Samuel got almost all the questions <u>right</u>.

    Ⓓ    Samuel got almost all the questions <u>wright</u>.


**4**    In which sentence are the underlined words used correctly?

    Ⓐ    The <u>road</u> was wet and slippery after the <u>rain</u>.

    Ⓑ    The <u>road</u> was wet and slippery after the <u>reign</u>.

    Ⓒ    The <u>rode</u> was wet and slippery after the <u>rain</u>.

    Ⓓ    The <u>rode</u> was wet and slippery after the <u>reign</u>.

## Quiz 43: Use Homographs

Homographs are words that are spelled the same, but have different meanings. For example, the word *rock* can refer to a type of music, a stone, or can mean "to sway." For each word below, write two sentences. Use a different meaning of the word in each sentence.

**1**  beat  1. _____

2. _____

**2**  bolt  1. _____

2. _____

**3**  plot  1. _____

2. _____

**4**  play  1. _____

2. _____

**5**  fair  1. _____

2. _____

## Quiz 44: Use Correct Punctuation

**1**  Which sentence has correct punctuation?

Ⓐ  Do you know which way the museum is?

Ⓑ  I walked around the streets for hours?

Ⓒ  Are there tickets left for the movie.

Ⓓ  I like watching a good movie, with, my friends.

**2**  Which sentence has correct punctuation?

Ⓐ  I ordered bacon eggs and beans.

Ⓑ  The school flag is yellow, green, and blue.

Ⓒ  Aaron has, a dog, a cat, and a bird.

Ⓓ  My sister's names are Manny Carla and Donna.

**3**  Choose the answer that shows the correct punctuation.

Ⓐ  It was'nt as late as I thought.

Ⓑ  They're meeting us later.

Ⓒ  I am going over to Sams house.

Ⓓ  Im going to call Shane later.

**4**  Choose the answer that shows the correct punctuation.

Ⓐ  "It's getting late" Joy said.

Ⓑ  "What's the time?" Dee asked."

Ⓒ  "Hold on!" Sophie yelled."

Ⓓ  "Can you give me a lift?" Dion asked.

## Quiz 45: Use Correct Capitalization

1    Choose the answer that shows the correct capitalization.

   Ⓐ    Alex is going to a party on the Weekend.

   Ⓑ    The new bookstore is on south street.

   Ⓒ    The camp is being held in november.

   Ⓓ    Uncle Simon lives in Texas.


2    Choose the answer that shows the correct capitalization.

   Ⓐ    I like spending time in Central park.

   Ⓑ    The Empire state building has an interesting history.

   Ⓒ    My mother usually takes a Taxi to work.

   Ⓓ    The boat sailed down the Hudson River.


3    Choose the answer that shows the correct capitalization.

   Ⓐ    I set up a Party for my young cousins.

   Ⓑ    The grand canyon was an amazing sight.

   Ⓒ    My new brother Jerry was born last Friday.

   Ⓓ    I would like to visit the beaches of california.


4    Choose the answer that shows the correct capitalization.

   Ⓐ    My aunt is flying on southwest airlines.

   Ⓑ    There is a good bakery on Fourth avenue.

   Ⓒ    The Civil war lasted for many years.

   Ⓓ    The Statue of Liberty is known all around the world.

## Quiz 46: Write Complete Sentences

**Choose the word or words that correctly completes each sentence below.**

1      The sound of the bell was very _____.

    Ⓐ      ringing

    Ⓑ      loud

    Ⓒ      hear it

    Ⓓ      in the tower


2      We went for a long hike _____.

    Ⓐ      morning

    Ⓑ      fitness

    Ⓒ      in the woods

    Ⓓ      got tired


3      Every plane that Damon made was _____.

    Ⓐ      perfect

    Ⓑ      nice paper

    Ⓒ      flew well

    Ⓓ      folded the paper


4      The painting was so beautiful that people sometimes stared at it _____.

    Ⓐ      admired

    Ⓑ      for hours

    Ⓒ      art gallery

    Ⓓ      very special

## Quiz 47: Combine Sentences

**1**  Which sentence best combines the two sentences?

**I didn't enjoy the book.**
**I stopped reading it.**

Ⓐ   I didn't enjoy the book, but I stopped reading it.

Ⓑ   I didn't enjoy the book, and I stopped reading it.

Ⓒ   I didn't enjoy the book, so I stopped reading it.

Ⓓ   I didn't enjoy the book, I stopped reading it.

**2**  Which sentence best combines the two sentences?

**Vienna opened her book.**
**Vienna started to read.**

Ⓐ   Vienna opened started to read her book.

Ⓑ   Vienna opened her book and started to read.

Ⓒ   Vienna started to open her book and read.

Ⓓ   Vienna opened her book started to read.

**3**  Which sentence best combines the two sentences?

**Allan studied math for an hour.**
**Then Allan studied science.**

Ⓐ   Allan studied math for an hour, and then studied science.

Ⓑ   Allan studied math and science for an hour.

Ⓒ   Allan studied math for an hour, then science.

Ⓓ   Allan studied for an hour, math and then science.

## Quiz 48: Identify Complete Sentences

**1**  Which sentence contains two complete thoughts and should be written as two sentences?

Ⓐ    The bookstore was busy, I bought two books.

Ⓑ    After lunch, we played a game of football.

Ⓒ    The shoes were very dear, so I didn't buy them.

Ⓓ    After I finished reading, I turned out the light.

**2**  Which sentence contains two complete thoughts and should be written as two sentences?

Ⓐ    It is hot in summer, but I like it.

Ⓑ    Next month, it will be my birthday.

Ⓒ    Even though it was late, I could not sleep.

Ⓓ    It rained all morning, it cleared up in the afternoon.

**3**  Which of these is NOT a complete sentence?

Ⓐ    I learned a new song.

Ⓑ    I sang it well.

Ⓒ    The crowd cheered.

Ⓓ    Felt good about myself.

**4**  Which of these is NOT a complete sentence?

Ⓐ    Kent got a new bike.

Ⓑ    Was bright blue and shiny.

Ⓒ    He liked it very much.

Ⓓ    The bike was looked after well.

## Quiz 49: Order Adjectives in Sentences

**For each sentence below, place the two given adjectives in the sentence in the best order.**

1    bossy        old

The _____ _____ man told us to get off his lawn.


2    red          lovely

Jerry bought his wife a bunch of _____ _____ roses.


3    relaxing     nice

We had a _____ _____ picnic in the park.


4    strange      creepy

We raced out of the _____ _____ house.


5    friendly     young

Oliver is a _____ _____ man.


6    broken       ugly

I decided to throw out the _____ _____ chair.

# Quiz 50: Understand and Use Similes and Metaphors

**1**   If Mark and Tierra are like two peas in a pod, they

Ⓐ   fight a lot

Ⓑ   are similar

Ⓒ   live in the same place

Ⓓ   are sharing a meal


**2**   If Chan moved like lightning, he moved

Ⓐ   in a dangerous way

Ⓑ   in a careful way

Ⓒ   in a quick way

Ⓓ   in a strange way


**3**   If Carrie's worries melted away, she

Ⓐ   worried less

Ⓑ   began to worry

Ⓒ   shared her worries

Ⓓ   worried for a long time


**4**   Which words complete the sentence below to show that the exam was easy?

**The students _____ the exam.**

Ⓐ   bowed out of

Ⓑ   plodded on through

Ⓒ   brushed aside

Ⓓ   sailed through

# ANSWER KEY

The Language Arts Florida Standards (LAFS) are a set of standards that describe what students are expected to know. Student learning throughout the year is based on these standards, and the Florida Standards Assessment (FSA) determines whether students have the skills described in the standards. All the exercises and questions in this book cover the skills listed in the Language Arts Florida Standards.

Each question in Section 1 of this book is based on one language skill described in the standards. The answer key identifies the skill covered by each question. In Section 2, each quiz is focused specifically on one skill listed in the standards. Additional information on the Language Arts Florida Standards is included at the end of the answer key.

# Section 1: Revising and Editing Quizzes

## Set 1

### Quiz 1

| Question | Answer | Language Skill |
|---|---|---|
| 1 | See Below | Choose words and phrases to convey ideas |
| 2 | A | Understand the meaning of suffixes |
| 3 | B | Understand the use of pronouns |
| 4 | B | Identify and use synonyms |
| 5 | B | Edit sentences for correctness |

Q1.  The student should explain that the phrase suggests that Kensi feels annoyed or angry. The student may explain that the words "slammed down" shows that she used a lot of force.

### Quiz 2

| Question | Answer | Language Skill |
|---|---|---|
| 1 | See Below | Understand the meaning of idioms |
| 2 | C | Use correct capitalization |
| 3 | B | Understand the meaning of phrases |
| 4 | B | Identify complete sentences |
| 5 | C | Edit sentences for correctness |

Q1.  The student should give the meanings below:
  - to call it a day: to finish or end
  - to be under the weather: to be sick or to feel unwell
  - to be a pain in the neck: to be annoying

### Quiz 3

| Question | Answer | Language Skill |
|---|---|---|
| 1 | A | Combine sentences correctly |
| 2 | B | Revise passages for clarity and relevance |
| 3 | C | Use context to determine word meaning |
| 4 | A | Use transition words and phrases effectively |
| 5 | B | Revise passages for organization |

## Quiz 4

| Question | Answer | Language Skill |
|:---:|:---:|:---:|
| 1 | See Below | Identify different types of words (adjectives) |
| 2 | D | Spell words correctly |
| 3 | B | Use correct verbs and correct verb tense |
| 4 | B | Identify different types of words (pronouns) |
| 5 | C | Identify literary techniques (simile) |

Q1.  The student should list the following adjectives:
- green, shady, modest, bent

## Quiz 5

| Question | Answer | Language Skill |
|:---:|:---:|:---:|
| 1 | See Below | Understand and use homonyms* |
| 2 | A | Revise sentences for clarity and coherence |
| 3 | B | Use correct punctuation (dates) |
| 4 | A | Spell words correctly |
| 5 | D | Use correct capitalization |

*Homonyms are words that have the same spelling and are pronounced the same, but have different meanings.

Q1.  The student should complete the table with the following words:
- yard, pound, inch

# Set 2

### Quiz 6

| Question | Answer | Language Skill |
|---|---|---|
| 1 | See Below | Choose words and phrases to convey ideas |
| 2 | B | Use transition words effectively |
| 3 | B | Use correct punctuation (dialogue) |
| 4 | D | Revise sentences for clarity and coherence |
| 5 | C | Use correct punctuation (commas) |

Q1.  The student should explain that the phrase "slumped over" suggests that Noah feels tired or worn out, and that the phrase "storming toward" suggests that Noah feels annoyed, angry, or determined.

### Quiz 7

| Question | Answer | Language Skill |
|---|---|---|
| 1 | C | Understand Greek and Latin word parts |
| 2 | B | Spell words correctly |
| 3 | B | Use correct subject-verb agreement |
| 4 | A | Choose words and phrases to convey ideas |
| 5 | D | Determine the meaning of words with multiple meanings |

### Quiz 8

| Question | Answer | Language Skill |
|---|---|---|
| 1 | See Below | Understand the meaning of idioms |
| 2 | B | Use correct verbs and correct verb tense |
| 3 | B | Spell words correctly |
| 4 | A | Write complete sentences |

Q1.  The student should explain that the phrase "not going to let anything stand in her way" means that Marcy is not going to let anything stop her.

## Quiz 9

| Question | Answer | Language Skill |
|---|---|---|
| 1 | See Below | Use contractions correctly |
| 2 | D | Understand the meaning of prefixes |
| 3 | A | Use correct punctuation (end punctuation) |
| 4 | B | Use correct capitalization and punctuation |
| 5 | B | Use correct punctuation (dates) |

Q1.   The student should write the following long form of each contraction:
- do not, cannot, was not, we will or we shall

## Quiz 10

| Question | Answer | Language Skill |
|---|---|---|
| 1 | B | Edit sentences for grammar and mechanics |
| 2 | D | Revise sentences for clarity and coherence |
| 3 | B | Determine the meaning of words based on word parts |
| 4 | C | Use context to determine word meaning |
| 5 | B | Identify correct complex sentences |

# Set 3

### Quiz 11

| Question | Answer | Language Skill |
|---|---|---|
| 1 | See Below | Understand and use literary techniques (alliteration) |
| 2 | A | Identify complete and incomplete sentences |
| 3 | A | Identify different types of words (pronouns) |
| 4 | B | Spell words correctly |
| 5 | B | Determine the meaning of words with multiple meanings |

Q1. The student should list the examples "star-sprinkled sky" and "wondering why." The student should give two additional examples of alliteration.

### Quiz 12

| Question | Answer | Language Skill |
|---|---|---|
| 1 | A | Use correct verbs and correct verb tense |
| 2 | B | Understand the meaning of idioms |
| 3 | A | Understand the meaning of suffixes |
| 4 | D | Combine sentences correctly |

### Quiz 13

| Question | Answer | Language Skill |
|---|---|---|
| 1 | C | Revise passages for organization |
| 2 | B | Use correct capitalization |
| 3 | B | Edit sentences for correctness |
| 4 | B | Revise sentences for clarity and coherence |
| 5 | D | Choose a relevant topic sentence |

**Quiz 14**

| Question | Answer | Language Skill |
|:---:|:---:|:---:|
| 1 | See Below | Understand and analyze word choices |
| 2 | C | Use correct punctuation (end punctuation) |
| 3 | C | Use context to determine word meaning |
| 4 | D | Revise sentences for clarity and correctness |
| 5 | D | Edit sentences for correctness |

Q1. The student may explain that the word *lurking* refers to moving around in a sneaky way. The student may explain that the author uses the word *lurking* to make the monster seem sneaky, scary, or dangerous.

**Quiz 15**

| Question | Answer | Language Skill |
|:---:|:---:|:---:|
| 1 | See Below | Understand and use homophones* |
| 2 | A | Understand the meaning of suffixes |
| 3 | D | Identify words with silent letters |
| 4 | A | Use correct verbs and correct verb tense |
| 5 | A | Use correct punctuation (apostrophes) |

*Homophones are words that are pronounced the same but have different meanings, such as the words *ate* and *eight*.

Q1. The student should give a correct definition of the word *piece*, such as "a part of something." The student should write a sentence that uses the word *piece* correctly.

# Set 4

**Quiz 16**

| Question | Answer | Language Skill |
|---|---|---|
| 1 | See Below | Spell words correctly |
| 2 | C | Use correct capitalization |
| 3 | C | Determine the meaning of words with multiple meanings |
| 4 | B | Understand the meaning of suffixes |
| 5 | C | Use correct punctuation (end punctuation) |

Q1.  The student should complete the sentences with the following words:
- photo or photograph, four, farm, phone, frog, feathers

**Quiz 17**

| Question | Answer | Language Skill |
|---|---|---|
| 1 | C | Use relative pronouns |
| 2 | D | Use phonics to identify and compare word sounds |
| 3 | C | Revise sentences for clarity and coherence |
| 4 | A | Use correct subject-verb agreement |
| 5 | B | Spell words with suffixes correctly |

**Quiz 18**

| Question | Answer | Language Skill |
|---|---|---|
| 1 | See Below | Use correct forms of plurals |
| 2 | A | Understand the meaning of abbreviations |
| 3 | B | Identify and use synonyms |
| 4 | D | Spell words with suffixes correctly |
| 5 | C | Revise sentences for clarity and coherence |

Q1.  The student should list the plural forms below:
- bikes, mice, shells, dresses, beaches, men, foxes, leaves, eagles, knives

**Quiz 19**

| Question | Answer | Language Skill |
|:---:|:---:|:---:|
| 1 | See Below | Divide words into syllables |
| 2 | B | Use correct verbs and correct verb tense |
| 3 | C | Use correct capitalization |
| 4 | B | Use irregular verbs |
| 5 | D | Identify and use synonyms |

Q1. The student should divide the words into syllables as below:

- con / cert, tick / et, con / test, big / gest, prob / lem, a / dored, mu / sic

**Quiz 20**

| Question | Answer | Language Skill |
|:---:|:---:|:---:|
| 1 | See Below | Understand and use homonyms* |
| 2 | B | Understand the meaning of prefixes |
| 3 | C | Understand and use adverbial phrases |
| 4 | B | Revise passages for organization |
| 5 | B | Choose a relevant topic sentence |

*Homonyms are words that have the same spelling and are pronounced the same, but have different meanings.

Q1. The student should give a meaning of *spot* other than "see or notice" and should write a sentence that uses the definition of *spot* given. Possible definitions are listed below:

- a small round area, a stain, a pimple, a place or location, a small amount, to stain something, to add dots to something

# Section 2: Language, Vocabulary, and Grammar Quizzes

### Quiz 21: Analyze Words
1. A
2. C
3. C
4. C

### Quiz 22: Identify and Use Antonyms
1. girl
2. tiny
3. cry
4. asleep
5. soft
6. last
7. new
8. inside
9. deep
10. tidy or clean

### Quiz 23: Understand the Meaning of Idioms
1. A
2. C
3. D
4. B

### Quiz 24: Use Modal Verbs Correctly
1. B
2. A
3. B
4. A

### Quiz 25: Use Words with Suffixes
1. D
2. A
3. B
4. C

### Quiz 26: Spell Commonly Misspelled Words
1. because
2. until
3. really
4. favorite
5. different
6. another

## Quiz 27: Understand and Use Prefixes
1. C
2. C
3. A
4. B

## Quiz 28: Understand and Use Suffixes
1. B
2. D
3. B
4. B

## Quiz 29: Understand Greek and Latin Word Parts
1. B
2. A
3. A
4. B

## Quiz 30: Spell Words with Suffixes Correctly
1. B
2. D
3. A
4. B

## Quiz 31: Use Contractions
1. he's
2. I'll
3. that'd
4. where's
5. we're
6. shouldn't

## Quiz 32: Use Prepositions
1. B
2. C
3. D
4. A

## Quiz 33: Identify Proper Nouns
1. Miss Williams taught us about the Cold War.
2. The Rocky Mountains are in North America.
3. My friend Amanda can speak Spanish.
4. My cousin Charlie lives in Alaska.
5. It can get really hot during June and July.
6. My mother is French, but she grew up in Miami.

## Quiz 34: Use Verbs Correctly
1. B
2. A
3. C

## Quiz 35: Use Correct Verb Tense
1. B
2. B
3. C
4. D

## Quiz 36: Use Correct Subject-Verb Agreement
1. B
2. B
3. C
4. C

## Quiz 37: Use Pronouns
1. C
2. C
3. C

## Quiz 38: Use Adverbs
Answers may vary for questions 2 through 5. Sample answers are given below, but any adverb that makes sense in the sentence can be accepted.
1. nicely
2. quickly
3. clearly
4. carefully
5. quietly
6. once
7. never
8. every
9. always
10. often

## Quiz 39: Spell Words Correctly
1. B
2. D
3. D
4. B

## Quiz 40: Choose Words or Phrases to Complete Sentences
1. B
2. A
3. A
4. D

## Quiz 41: Use Context to Determine Word Meanings
1. D
2. A
3. C

## Quiz 42: Use Frequently Confused Words
1. D
2. C
3. C
4. A

## Quiz 43: Use Homographs
Answers may vary. Sample answers are given below.
1. I danced to the beat. / I beat my friend at chess.
2. I saw Mike bolt away. / The bolt on the door was stuck.
3. The book had a good plot. / We planted corn in the plot.
4. We went to the park to play. / Many people tried out for the school play.
5. There were rides at the fair. / I have very fair skin.

## Quiz 44: Use Correct Punctuation
1. A
2. B
3. B
4. D

## Quiz 45: Use Correct Capitalization
1. D
2. D
3. C
4. D

## Quiz 46: Write Complete Sentences
1. B
2. C
3. A
4. B

## Quiz 47: Combine Sentences
1. C
2. B
3. A

## Quiz 48: Identify Complete Sentences
1. A
2. D
3. D
4. B

## Quiz 49: Order Adjectives in Sentences
1. bossy old
2. lovely red
3. nice relaxing
4. strange creepy
5. friendly young
6. ugly broken

## Quiz 50: Understand and Use Similes and Metaphors
1. B
2. C
3. A
4. D

# LANGUAGE ARTS FLORIDA STANDARDS
# For Parents, Teachers, and Tutors

The Language Arts Florida Standards describe what students are expected to be able to do. Student learning is based on these standards throughout the year. The standards are divided into the following four areas: Reading, Writing, Speaking and Listening, and Language.

The content of this quiz book is focused mainly on the Language standards. However, parts of the Reading and Writing standards are also covered. The Reading, Writing, and Language standards covered in this quiz book are listed below.

## Reading Standards: Foundational Skills

*The Foundational Skills listed as part of the Reading standards describe the basic conventions of English that students need to read and comprehend texts. These skills are covered by some of the questions in Section 1 of this book and by some of the quizzes in Section 2 of this book. The standards covered are listed below.*

**Know and apply grade-level phonics and word analysis skills in decoding words.**
a. Use combined knowledge of all letter-sound correspondences, syllabication patterns, and morphology (e.g., roots and affixes) to read accurately unfamiliar multisyllabic words in context and out of context.

**Read with sufficient accuracy and fluency to support comprehension.**
a. Read on-level text with purpose and understanding.
b. Read on-level prose and poetry orally with accuracy, appropriate rate, and expression on successive readings.
c. Use context to confirm or self-correct word recognition and understanding, rereading as necessary.

## Writing Standards

*The Writing standards describe the production of writing, as well as the editing and revising of writing. The questions in Section 1 of this book cover the editing and revising standard below.*

With guidance and support from peers and adults, develop and strengthen writing as needed by planning, revising, and editing. (Editing for conventions should demonstrate command of Language standards.)

# Language Standards

*The Language standards describe the grammar, language, and vocabulary skills expected of students. The questions in Section 1 of this book require students to apply these skills, while the quizzes in Section 2 focus specifically on developing and improving these skills. The Language standards are listed below.*

**Demonstrate command of the conventions of standard English grammar and usage when writing or speaking.**
a. Demonstrate legible cursive writing skills.
b. Use relative pronouns (who, whose, whom, which, that) and relative adverbs (where, when, why).
c. Form and use the progressive verb tenses.
d. Use modal auxiliaries (e.g., can, may, must) to convey various conditions.
e. Order adjectives within sentences according to conventional patterns.
f. Form and use prepositional phrases.
g. Produce complete sentences, recognizing and correcting inappropriate fragments and run-ons.
h. Correctly use frequently confused words (e.g., to, too, two; there, their).

**Demonstrate command of the conventions of standard English capitalization, punctuation, and spelling when writing.**
a. Use correct capitalization.
b. Use commas and quotation marks to mark direct speech and quotations from a text.
c. Use a comma before a coordinating conjunction in a compound sentence.
d. Spell grade-appropriate words correctly, consulting references as needed.

**Use knowledge of language and its conventions when writing, speaking, reading, or listening.**
a. Choose words and phrases to convey ideas precisely.
b. Choose punctuation for effect.
c. Differentiate between contexts that call for formal English (e.g., presenting ideas) and situations where informal discourse is appropriate (e.g., small-group discussion).

**Determine or clarify the meaning of unknown and multiple-meaning words and phrases based on grade 4 reading and content, choosing flexibly from an array of strategies.**
a. Use context as a clue to the meaning of a word or phrase.
b. Use common, grade-appropriate Greek and Latin affixes and roots as clues to the meaning of a word.
c. Consult reference materials (e.g., dictionaries, glossaries, thesauruses), both print and digital, to find the pronunciation and determine or clarify the precise meaning of key words and phrases.

**Demonstrate understanding of figurative language, word relationships, and nuances in word meanings.**

a. Explain the meaning of simple similes and metaphors in context.

b. Recognize and explain the meaning of common idioms, adages, and proverbs.

c. Demonstrate understanding of words by relating them to their opposites (antonyms) and to words with similar but not identical meanings (synonyms).

**Acquire and use accurately general academic and domain-specific words and phrases as found in grade level appropriate texts, including those that signal precise actions, emotions, or states of being.**

CPSIA information can be obtained at www.ICGtesting.com
Printed in the USA
LVOW09s1025170316

479577LV00006B/124/P

9 781500 971342